cocktails

cocktails

TIME
LIFE
BOOKS

Alexandria, Virginia

Time-Life Books is a division of Time Life Inc.

TIME LIFE INC.
Chairman and CEO   Jim Nelson
President and COO   Steven L. Janas

TIME-LIFE TRADE PUBLISHING
Vice President and Publisher   Neil Levin
Senior Director of Acquisitions and Editorial Resources Jennifer Pearce
Director of New Product Development   Carolyn Clark
Director of Marketing   Inger Forland
Director of Trade Sales   Dana Hobson
Director of Custom Publishing   John Lalor
Director of Special Markets   Robert Lombardi
Director of Design   Kate L. McConnell

COCKTAILS
Project Manager   Jennie Halfant
Technical Specialist   Monika Lynde

This edition first published in the U.K. in 1999 by Hamlyn
Octopus Publishing Group Limited
2–4 Heron Quays
London E14 4JP

Printed in China
10 9 8 7 6 5 4 3 2 1

TIME-LIFE is a trademark of Time Warner Inc. and affiliated companies.

Library of Congress Cataloging-in-Publication Data
Cocktails: over 70 simple recipes for elegant cocktails.
     p. cm.
   Includes index.
   ISBN 0-7370-2052-0
     1. Cocktails. I. Time-Life Books.

   TX951 .C62 2000
   641.8'74--dc21
                                              00-023454

Notes
1 Milk should be whole milk unless otherwise stated.
2 The measure that has been used in the cocktail recipes is based on a bar jigger, which is 1½ fl oz.
If preferred, a different volume can be used providing the proportions are kept constant within a
drink, and suitable adjustments are made to spoon measurements, where they occur.

contents

6

introduction

Cocktails are pure escapism. Short mixed drinks—usually alcohol-based—are made to an exact recipe rather than poured in a haphazard fashion, which is one of the reasons for their deceptively powerful kick. They can also, though this is a very modern trend, be non-alcoholic.

Despite their association with the bright young things of the 1920s, cocktails have been around for a long time. Mixed drinks were popular in the nineteenth century, and the use of the word cocktail goes back to 1806, or 1809, depending upon which reference book you prefer. Daisies, cobblers, and fixes are all part of Victorian drinking history, whereas punch goes back even further, to the eighteenth century. As well as having their own bar equipment and glasses, cocktails have their own language. Among the best-known names, a cobbler is a wine-based mixed drink, originally made with sherry; sours are mixtures of spirit, lemon, and sugar, and daisies are similar to sours but with the addition of a sweet syrup.

Juleps, long drinks made with bourbon and mint, are part of the history of the Deep South, and it is impossible to enjoy a really well-made julep without succumbing to fantasies of a lifestyle with overtones of *Gone With the Wind*. Captain Marryat (1792–1848), better known for his adventure stories such as *Mr Midshipman Easy* and *The Children of the New Forest*, felt that mint juleps were the perfect drink for when the temperature was 100°F but grudgingly conceded that they were still enjoyable at 70°F! The Collinses (see page 37) are another American drink, while slings, sweetish long drinks, which are usually with a gin base, are associated with colonial life in the Far East. Eggnogs have long been popular on both sides of the Atlantic and are traditionally served at Christmas.

The word punch is said to come from *panch*, the Hindustani word for five, and refers to the five elements in punch (alcohol, citrus, sugar, spice, and water). However, the classic formula for a rum punch in the West Indies "One of sour, two of sweet, three of strong and four of weak"—contains only four elements, being made without spice. (The sour element is a lime slice, the sweet is syrup, the strong is rum and the weak is water.)

Glasses

There is no reason why many cocktails shouldn't be served in a standard wine glass, which holds 5 fl oz. However, there is no doubt that using the classic shaped cocktail glass or the curiously shaped Margarita glass adds to the pleasure of the occasion; old fashioned glasses are convenient for a short drink on the rocks, whereas for longer drinks a highball glass, a hurricane glass, or the even taller Collins glass are most suitable. Hot punches should be served in a mug or a heatproof glass with a handle.

Bar Equipment

The basic pieces of bar equipment for the serious bartender are a cocktail shaker, a mixing glass, and a blender. The shaker, which usually comes with a built-in strainer, is for drinks that contain ingredients such as eggs, cream, thick liqueurs, and slices or chunks of fruit, which need a really thorough shake to blend all the elements. The mixing glass (actually large enough to contain several drinks) is for drinks that are just stirred together. It is used in conjunction with a long bar spoon and then strained or poured directly into glasses. The blender is for smoothies and other drinks made with ice cream and fruit.

A set of bar measures ensures absolute accuracy and saves a lot of time, and a coil-rimmed bar strainer is also helpful. Other important pieces of bar equipment, most of which will be found in any kitchen, are a lemon squeezer, a paring knife and chopping board, ice cube trays and ice buckets, teaspoons and tablespoons, and, of course, corkscrews and bottle openers, towels and cocktail sticks. A waiter's corkscrew is a useful gadget to have on hand in case corks prove stubborn. Teaspoons and tablespoons should be kept in a jug of water when not in use so that they are rinsed between mixes.

Ice

Ice is essential for a well-made cocktail, so always make sure that you have plenty available when you are making drinks. When ice is added to a shaker, it acts as a beater as well as cooling the mixture. Use tongs rather than a spoon for putting ice into drinks, so that you don't add cold water with the ice cubes. Sometimes recipes ask for cracked ice or crushed ice. To make cracked ice put a handful of ice cubes into a strong plastic bag and hit them with a rolling pin. For crushed ice, simply go on hitting the ice for a little longer.

Sugar Syrup

Sugar syrup is used in many cocktails as it is easier to stir into cold drinks than sugar. To make up a supply, combine equal quantities of sugar and water and bring them to a boil in a small saucepan, stirring until the sugar is dissolved, then boil for 1 minute without stirring. Sugar syrup can be stored in a sterilized bottle in the refrigerator for up to 2 months.

"Let's get out of these wet clothes
and into a dry Martini."

Alexander Woollcott

Decorating Cocktails

A cocktail looks good with a decorative finish. Traditional decorations include slices
of lemon, orange, lime or cucumber, twists of citrus zest, maraschino cherries, and
green olives. Herbs, especially mint, add flavor as well as looking attractive. Long
thin spirals of lemon or orange rind are an up-to-date touch, as are strawberries,
whole or halved, and other pieces of fruit, including pineapple and mango. Glass
swizzle sticks and tiny paper parasols make an attractive finishing touch and can
save you time if you are mixing drinks on your own. Ice cubes frozen with sprigs of
herbs, mint is a favorite, or raspberries, look most attractive and can be prepared
well in advance to save time.

gin

dry martini

Put the ice cubes into a mixing glass. Pour the vermouth and gin over the ice and stir (never shake) vigorously and evenly, without splashing, then strain into a chilled cocktail glass. Serve with a green olive and a straw.

Pictured Left

5–6 ice cubes

1½ teaspoons dry vermouth

2 measures gin

1 green olive

Serves 1
Preparation time: 3 minutes

The Dry Martini, which was invented at the Knickerbocker Hotel in New York in 1910, has become the most famous cocktail of all. Lemon zest is sometimes used as a decoration instead of a green olive.

burnsides

Put 4–5 ice cubes into a cocktail shaker. Shake the bitters over the ice, add the cherry brandy, the sweet and dry vermouths, and the gin. Shake lightly, then strain into a glass over the remaining ice cubes. Decorate with lemon zest strips.

Pictured Right

8–10 ice cubes

2 drops Angostura bitters

1 teaspoon cherry brandy

1 measure sweet vermouth

2 measures dry vermouth

2 measures gin

lemon zest strips

Serves 1
Preparation time: 3 minutes

sapphire martini

Put the ice cubes into a cocktail shaker. Pour in the gin and blue Curaçao, and shake well to mix. Strain into a chilled cocktail glass and carefully drop in the blue cocktail cherry, if using.

4–5 ice cubes

2 measures gin

½ measure blue Curaçao

1 blue cocktail cherry (optional)

Serves 1

Preparation time: 2 minutes

■ A Salty Dog can also be made with vodka. Sometimes the glass is rimmed with salt, like a Margarita.

2–3 ice cubes
pinch of salt
1 measure gin
2–2½ measures fresh grapefruit juice
orange slice, to decorate

Put the ice cubes into an old fashioned glass. Put the salt on the ice and add the gin and grapefruit juice. Stir gently and serve. Decorate with an orange slice.

Serves 1
Preparation time: 2 minutes

salty dog

morning glory fizz

Put the ice cubes into a cocktail shaker. Pour the lemon juice, sugar syrup, and gin over the ice. Add the egg white, then the Pernod, and shake until a frost forms. Strain into a chilled old fashioned glass, top up with ginger ale, and serve with a straw.

4–5 ice cubes

1 measure fresh lemon juice

½ teaspoon sugar syrup

3 measures gin

1 egg white

3 drops Pernod

ginger ale

Serves 1

Preparation time: 4 minutes

4–5 ice cubes

juice of ½ lemon

1 measure cherry brandy

3 measures gin

club soda

cherries, to decorate (optional)

Serves 2

Preparation time: 3 minutes

Put the ice cubes into a cocktail shaker. Pour the lemon juice, cherry brandy, and gin over the ice, and shake until a frost forms. Pour without straining into a hurricane glass and top up with club soda. Decorate with cherries, if you like, and serve with straws.

gin sling

ben's orange cream

Put the ice cubes into a cocktail shaker. Pour the Cointreau, cream, and gin over the ice. Add the sugar syrup to the gin mixture and shake until a frost forms. Pour into a large glass and decorate with grated chocolate.

Pictured Left

4–5 ice cubes

1 measure Cointreau

1 measure light cream

3 measures gin

1 tablespoon sugar syrup

grated chocolate, to decorate

Serves 2

Preparation time: 4 minutes

lime gin fizz

Put the ice cubes into a tall glass. Pour the gin and the lime cordial over the ice cubes. Top up with club soda, decorate with wedges of lime, and serve with straws.

Pictured Right

4–5 ice cubes

2 measures gin

1 measure lime cordial

club soda

lime wedges, to decorate

Serves 1

Preparation time: 3 minutes

clover club

Put the ice cubes into a cocktail shaker. Pour the lime juice, sugar syrup, egg white, and gin over the ice, and shake until a frost forms. Strain into a tumbler and serve decorated with grated lime zest and a lime wedge.

4–5 ice cubes

juice of 1 lime

½ teaspoon sugar syrup

1 egg white

3 measures gin

To Decorate:

grated lime zest

lime wedge

Serves 1

Preparation time: 3 minutes

4–5 ice cubes

juice of 1 lime

dash of grenadine

1 egg white

3 measures gin

strawberry slice, to decorate

Put the ice cubes into a cocktail shaker. Pour the lime juice, grenadine, egg white, and gin over the ice. Shake until a frost forms, then strain into a cocktail glass. Decorate with a strawberry slice and serve with a straw.

Serves 1
Preparation time: 3 minutes

pink clover club

Grenadine is a sweet non-alcoholic syrup made from pomegranates, which give it its rich rosy pink color.

gin cup

Put the mint and sugar syrup into an old fashioned glass and stir them around to bruise the mint slightly. Fill the glass with chopped ice, add the lemon juice and gin, and stir until a frost begins to form. Decorate with extra mint sprigs.

3 mint sprigs plus extra to decorate

1 teaspoon sugar syrup

chopped ice

juice of ½ lemon

3 measures gin

Serves 1

Preparation time: 4 minutes

4–5 ice cubes

1 measure fresh lemon juice

1 measure fresh orange juice

½ teaspoon grenadine

3 measures gin

3 drops Angostura bitters

club soda

orange slice, to decorate

Serves 1
Preparation time: 4 minutes

Put the ice cubes into a cocktail shaker. Pour in the lemon juice, orange juice, grenadine, and gin. Add the bitters and shake until a frost forms. Pour into a tall glass and top up with club soda. Decorate with a slice of orange and serve with straws.

alice springs

maiden's prayer

Put the ice cubes into a cocktail shaker. Pour the bitters over the ice, add the lemon juice, Cointreau, and gin, and shake until a frost forms. Strain into a cocktail glass and serve with a straw.

Pictured Left

4–5 ice cubes

3 drops Angostura bitters

juice of 1 lemon

1 measure Cointreau

2 measures gin

Serves 1

Preparation time: 4 minutes

knockout

Put the ice cubes into a mixing glass. Pour the vermouth, crème de menthe, and gin over the ice, stir vigorously, then strain into a chilled old fashioned glass. Add the Pernod and serve with a lemon slice.

Pictured Right

4–5 ice cubes

1 measure dry vermouth

½ measure white crème de menthe

2 measures gin

1 drop Pernod

lemon slice, to serve

Serves 1

Preparation time: 4 minutes

Crème de menthe is a sweetish mint-flavored liqueur, which may be green or white in color, although the flavor remains the same. The white version is used here to blend with the milky color of the Pernod.

whiskey

whiskey milk punch

Put the ice cubes into a cocktail shaker. Pour the sugar syrup, whiskey, and milk over the ice, and shake until a frost forms. Pour without straining into an old fashioned glass, sprinkle with grated nutmeg, and serve.

Pictured Left

4–5 ice cubes

1 teaspoon sugar syrup

2 measures whiskey

3 measures milk

grated nutmeg

Serves 1
Preparation time: 3 minutes

golden daisy

Put the ice cubes into a cocktail shaker. Pour the lemon juice, sugar syrup, Cointreau, and whiskey over the ice and shake vigorously until a frost forms. Strain into an old fashioned glass and serve decorated with a
lime wedge.

Pictured Right

4–5 ice cubes

juice of 1 lemon

1 teaspoon sugar syrup

½ measure Cointreau

3 measures whiskey

lime wedge, to decorate

Serves 1
Preparation time: 3 minutes

This is one of the drinks that dates back to the nineteenth century but seems surprisingly modern. Although daisies may also be made with gin or rum, the general feeling is that whiskey, especially bourbon, makes the best drink.

southerly buster

Put the ice cubes into a mixing glass. Pour the Curaçao and whiskey over the ice, stir vigorously, then strain into chilled cocktail glasses. Twist the lemon rind over the drinks and drop it in. Serve with a straw.

4–5 ice cubes

1 measure blue Curaçao

3 measures whiskey

2 pieces of lemon rind

Serves 2

Preparation time: 3 minutes

4–5 ice cubes

juice of 1 lemon

juice of ½ orange

½ teaspoon grenadine

3 measures Scotch

Serves 1

Preparation time: 4 minutes

Put the ice cubes into a mixing glass. Pour the lemon juice, orange juice, grenadine, and Scotch over the ice. Stir vigorously, then strain into a chilled cocktail glass. Serve with a straw.

scots guards

tar

Put the ice cubes into a cocktail shaker. Pour in the lemon juice, grenadine, crème de cacao, and Scotch. Shake until a frost forms, then strain into chilled cocktail glasses. Serve with a straw.

Pictured Left

4–5 ice cubes

juice of 1 lemon

½ teaspoon grenadine

1 measure crème de cacao

3 measures Scotch

Serves 2
Preparation time: 3 minutes

Crème de cacao is a chocolate liqueur available in a colorless version as well as a chocolate-colored one.

bunny hug

Put the ice cubes into a mixing glass. Pour the Pernod, gin, and Scotch over the ice, stir vigorously, then strain into chilled cocktail glasses. Serve with a straw.

Pictured Right

4–5 ice cubes

1 measure Pernod

1 measure gin

3 measures Scotch

Serves 2
Preparation time: 2 minutes

suburban

Put the ice cubes into a mixing glass. Shake the bitters over the ice, then pour in the port, rum, and bourbon or Scotch. Stir vigorously, then pour into a chilled old fashioned glass.

4–5 ice cubes

3 drops orange bitters or Angostura bitters

1 measure port

1 measure dark rum

3 measures bourbon or Scotch

Serves 2

Preparation time: 3 minutes

■ This cocktail takes its name from the Algonquin Hotel in New York, made famous by Dorothy Parker, James Thurber, and the other writers and artists of *The New Yorker* magazine.

4–5 ice cubes

1 measure unsweetened pineapple juice

1 measure dry vermouth

3 measures bourbon or Scotch

Serves 1

Preparation time: 3 minutes

Put the ice cubes into a mixing glass. Pour the pineapple juice, vermouth, and bourbon or Scotch over the ice. Stir vigorously, until nearly frothy, then strain into a chilled cocktail glass. Serve decorated with a cocktail parasol and drink with a straw.

algonquin

skipper

Put the ice cubes into a mixing glass. Pour the grenadine over the ice and add the orange juice, vermouth, and rye or Scotch. Stir vigorously, until nearly frothy, then pour into a tumbler. Decorate with an orange slice and serve with a straw.

4–5 ice cubes

4 drops grenadine

juice of ½ orange

1 measure dry vermouth

3 measures rye or Scotch

orange slice, to decorate

Serves 1

Preparation time: 3 minutes

The Collins is the longest and most refreshing of drinks—and there are Collinses made with just about every spirit. The Tom Collins is made with gin (in Britain it is called a John Collins), Sandy Collins is made with Scotch whisky, and Pierre Collins with brandy. The Rum Collins is made with dark rum and the Pedro Collins with white rum, whereas a Collins made with vodka is simply known as a Vodka Collins.

Put the ice cubes into a cocktail shaker. Pour the lemon juice, sugar syrup, and whiskey over the ice, and shake until a frost forms. Pour without straining into a tumbler or Collins glass, and add the orange slice and maraschino cherry speared on a cocktail stick. Top up with the club soda, stir lightly, and serve decorated with an orange zest spiral.

5–6 ice cubes
juice of 1 lemon
1 tablespoon sugar syrup
3 measures Irish whiskey
1 orange slice
1 maraschino cherry
club soda
orange zest spiral, to decorate

Serves 1

Preparation time: 4 minutes

mike collins

clear skies ahead

Put the ice cubes into a cocktail shaker. Pour in the sugar syrup, lemon juice, grenadine, egg white, and Scotch. Shake until a frost forms, then pour into an old fashioned glass. Serve decorated with a cocktail parasol.

Pictured Left

4–5 ice cubes

½ teaspoon sugar syrup

juice of ½ lemon

½ teaspoon grenadine

1 egg white

2 measures Scotch

Serves 1
Preparation time: 3 minutes

walters

Put the ice cubes into a mixing glass. Pour the lemon juice, orange juice, and bourbon or Scotch over the ice. Stir vigorously, then strain into a chilled old fashioned glass. Serve decorated with an orange slice. Drink with a straw.

Pictured Right

4–5 ice cubes

juice of ½ lemon

juice of ½ orange

3 measures bourbon or Scotch

orange slice, to decorate

Serves 1
Preparation time: 4 minutes

mint julep

Put the mint sprigs into an iced silver mug or tall glass. Add the sugar syrup, then crush the mint into the syrup with a teaspoon. Fill the mug or a glass with dry crushed ice, pour the bourbon over the ice, and stir gently. Pack in more crushed ice and stir until a frost forms. Wrap the mug or glass in a table napkin, and serve decorated with a mint sprig.

9 tender young mint sprigs plus extra to decorate

1 teaspoon sugar syrup

crushed ice

3 measures bourbon

Serves 1

Preparation time: 5 minutes

Making the perfect julep is a time-consuming business. Ideally it should be served in a silver mug that must be thoroughly chilled, if not iced. Second, only crushed ice that has been pounded and dried as much as possible should be used. Third, the mug mustn't be touched during the preparation otherwise the frost will disappear. If you haven't got a silver mug, use a tall glass instead.

crushed ice

3 drops Angostura bitters

1 teaspoon sugar syrup

juice of 1 lemon

1 measure brandy

1 measure dark rum

2 measures whiskey

Half-fill a tall glass with crushed ice. Shake the bitters over the ice. Pour in the sugar syrup and the lemon juice, then stir gently to mix thoroughly. Add the brandy, rum, and whiskey, in that order, stir once and serve with straws.

Serves 1
Preparation time: 3 minutes

mississippi punch

rum

½ lime

2 measures pineapple juice

1 measure light rum

1 teaspoon sugar

3–4 ice cubes

ginger ale

lime slice, to decorate

Serves 1
Preparation time: 4 minutes

Cut the lime into 4 pieces, put them into a blender or food processor, along with the pineapple juice, rum, and sugar, and blend until smooth. Put the ice into a hurricane glass or large goblet, pour in the drink, and top up with ginger ale. Decorate with the lime slice and serve with straws.

havana beach

batiste

Put the ice cubes into a mixing glass. Pour the Grand Marnier and rum over the ice, stir vigorously, then strain into a cocktail glass.

4–5 ice cubes

1 measure Grand Marnier

2 measures light or dark rum

Serves 1

Preparation time: 3 minutes

Grand Marnier is a brandy-based orange liqueur. It is made by a French liqueur company, hence its presence in this cocktail from one of the French speaking islands in the Caribbean.

pink rum

Shake the bitters into a highball glass and swirl them around. Add the ice cubes, then pour in the rum, cranberry juice, and club soda, and serve decorated with a lime slice.

Pictured Left

3 drops Angostura bitters

3–4 ice cubes

2 measures light rum

2 measures cranberry juice

1 measure club soda

lime slice, to decorate

Serves 1
Preparation time: 4 minutes

zombie christophe

Put the ice cubes into a mixing glass. Pour the lime or lemon juice, orange juice, pineapple juice, Curaçao, and light and golden rums over the ice. Stir vigorously, then pour without straining into a tumbler. Top with the dark rum, stir gently, and serve decorated with a lemon slice and a mint sprig.

Pictured Right

4–5 ice cubes

juice of 1 lime or lemon

juice of ½ orange

8 oz. unsweetened pineapple juice

1 measure blue Curaçao

1 measure light rum

1 measure golden rum

½ measure dark rum

To Decorate:

lime or lemon slice

mint sprig

Serves 1
Preparation time: 5 minutes

grenada

Put the ice cubes into a mixing glass. Pour the orange juice, vermouth, and rum over the ice. Stir vigorously, then strain into a chilled cocktail glass. Sprinkle a little ground cinnamon on top and serve.

4–5 ice cubes

juice of ½ orange

1 measure sweet vermouth

3 measures golden or dark rum

ground cinnamon

Serves 1

Preparation time: 4 minutes

Zombies contain all three types of rum—dark, golden, and light. The darker rums are aged in charred oak casks, whereas light rums are aged in stainless steel tanks.

crushed ice

juice of 1 lemon

juice of 1 orange

juice of ½ grapefruit

3 drops Angostura bitters

1 teaspoon soft brown sugar

1 measure light rum

1 measure golden rum

1 measure dark rum

Put the crushed ice into a mixing glass. Pour the lemon, orange, and grapefruit juices over the ice, and splash in the bitters. Add the sugar, and pour in the three rums. Stir vigorously, then pour without straining into a Collins glass. Decorate with lime and orange slices.

To Decorate:

lime slices

orange slices

Serves 1

Preparation time: 6 minutes

zombie prince

tobago fizz

Put the ice cubes into a cocktail shaker. Pour the lime or lemon juice, orange juice, rum, cream, and sugar syrup over the ice. Shake until a frost forms, then strain into a goblet. Top up with club soda, and serve decorated with an orange slice and a strawberry slice on a cocktail stick, and drink with straws.

4–5 ice cubes

juice of ½ lime or lemon

juice of ½ orange

3 measures golden rum

1 measure light cream

½ teaspoon sugar syrup

club soda

To Decorate:

orange slice

strawberry slice

Serves 1

Preparation time: 5 minutes

4–5 ice cubes

3 drops Angostura bitters

juice of ½ lime

1 teaspoon Curaçao or blue Curaçao

1 teaspoon sugar syrup

3 measures golden or dark rum

lime slices, to decorate

Serves 1
Preparation time: 4 minutes

Put the ice cubes into a cocktail shaker. Shake the bitters over the ice. Pour in the lime juice, Curaçao, sugar syrup, and rum, and shake until a frost forms. Strain into an old fashioned glass. Decorate with lime slices.

discovery bay

■ Curaçao comes from the Dutch Caribbean island of that name. It is produced in several colors including a vivid blue, but regardless of the color, it is always orange-flavored.

daiquiri

Put lots of cracked ice into a cocktail shaker. Pour the lime juice, sugar syrup, and rum over the ice. Shake thoroughly until a frost forms, then strain into a chilled cocktail glass.

cracked ice

juice of 2 limes

1 teaspoon sugar syrup

3 measures light rum

Serves 1

Preparation time: 4 minutes

The Daiquiri was created by an American mining engineer working in Cuba in 1896. He was expecting VIP guests and his supplies of gin had run out so he extemporized with rum—and created this classic cocktail.

1 measure light rum

½ measure crème de fraise

½ measure fresh lemon juice

4 ripe strawberries, hulled

crushed ice

To Decorate:

strawberry slice

mint sprig

Put the rum, crème de fraise, lemon juice, strawberries, and ice into a food processor or blender and blend at a slow speed for 5 seconds, then at high speed for about 20 seconds. Pour into a chilled glass and decorate with a strawberry slice and a mint sprig.

Serves 1

Preparation time: 5 minutes

strawberry daiquiri

punch julien

Pour the lime juice and pineapple juice into a mixing glass and shake in the bitters. Pour in the grenadine and golden and dark rums, and add the fruit. Stir thoroughly, then chill in the refrigerator for 3 hours. Fill an old fashioned glass with cracked ice. Pour the punch over the ice and add the fruit. Sprinkle with nutmeg and serve decorated with a pineapple wedge.

Pictured Left

juice of 2 limes

1 measure unsweetened pineapple juice

3 drops Angostura bitters

½ teaspoon grenadine

1 measure golden rum

3 measures dark rum

1 lime slice

1 lemon slice

1 orange slice

1 pineapple wedge plus extra to decorate

cracked ice

grated nutmeg

Serves 1

Preparation time: 6 minutes plus chilling

bahamas punch

Pour the lemon juice and sugar syrup into a mixing glass. Shake in the bitters, then add the grenadine, rum, and orange and lemon slices. Stir thoroughly and chill in the refrigerator for 3 hours. To serve, fill an old fashioned glass with cracked ice, pour in the punch without straining, and sprinkle with nutmeg.

Pictured Right

juice of 1 lemon

1 teaspoon sugar syrup

3 drops Angostura bitters

½ teaspoon grenadine

3 measures golden or light rum

1 orange slice

1 lemon slice

cracked ice

grated nutmeg

Serves 1

Preparation time: 5 minutes plus chilling

brandy

brandy manhattan

Put the ice cubes into a mixing glass. Pour the vermouth and brandy over the ice and stir vigorously. Pour into two chilled glasses and decorate each with a maraschino cherry.

4–5 ice cubes

1 measure sweet vermouth

3 measures brandy

2 maraschino cherries, to decorate

Serves 2

Preparation time: 3 minutes

This cocktail dates back to the First World War. It was made for a man who traveled to a Paris bar in a chauffeur-driven motorcycle sidecar.

4–5 ice cubes
juice of 1 lemon
1 measure Cointreau
2 measures brandy

To Decorate:
orange zest
maraschino cherry

Serves 1

Preparation time: 3 minutes

Put the ice cubes into a mixing glass. Pour the lemon juice, Cointreau, and brandy over the ice and stir vigorously. Strain into a chilled cocktail glass. Decorate with orange zest and a maraschino cherry on a cocktail stick.

brandy sidecar

brandy classic

Put the ice cubes into a cocktail shaker. Pour in the brandy, Curaçao, maraschino liqueur, and lemon juice, and shake together. Strain into a chilled cocktail glass. Add some cracked ice and a wedge of lemon and serve.

4–5 ice cubes

1 measure brandy

1 measure blue Curaçao

1 measure maraschino liqueur

juice of ½ lemon

cracked ice

lemon wedge, to serve

Serves 1

Preparation time: 3 minutes

■ Maraschino liqueur is a sweet cherry brandy made in Italy. Substitute another type of cherry brandy if you cannot find it.

crushed ice

1 teaspoon sugar syrup

juice of ½ lemon

½ measure cherry brandy

1 measure brandy

lemon slice, to serve

Serves 1

Preparation time: 3 minutes

Half-fill a tumbler with crushed ice.
Add the sugar syrup, lemon juice,
cherry brandy, and brandy, and stir.
Serve with a slice of lemon.

brandy fix

paradise

Put the ice cubes into a cocktail shaker. Add the lemon juice, orange juice, gin, and apricot brandy, and shake together. Strain into a chilled cocktail glass and decorate with slices of lemon and orange.

Pictured Left

4–5 ice cubes

1 dash fresh lemon juice

1 measure fresh orange juice

1 measure gin

1 measure apricot brandy

To Decorate:

lemon slice

orange slice

Serves 1

Preparation time: 4 minutes

heir apparent

Put the ice cubes into a mixing glass. Shake the bitters over the ice and pour in the brandy. Stir vigorously, then strain into a chilled cocktail glass. Add the crème de menthe and serve decorated with the mint sprig.

Pictured Right

4–5 ice cubes

3 drops orange bitters or Angostura bitters

3 measures brandy

3 drops white crème de menthe

mint sprig, to decorate

Serves 1

Preparation time: 3 minutes

eggnog

Half-fill a cocktail shaker with ice. Add the egg, sugar syrup, brandy, and milk, and shake well for about 1 minute. Strain into a tumbler and sprinkle with some grated nutmeg. Drink with a straw, if you like.

4–5 ice cubes

1 egg

1 tablespoon sugar syrup

2 measures brandy

5 oz. milk

grated nutmeg, to decorate

Serves 1

Preparation time: 4 minutes

Although eggnogs have a deceptively mild appearance, they are very potent, the Baltimore version in particular, so approach them with caution!

4–5 ice cubes

1 egg

1 tablespoon sugar syrup

½ measure brandy

½ measure dark rum

½ measure Madeira

2 measures milk

To Decorate:

ground cinnamon

cinnamon stick

Half-fill a cocktail shaker with ice cubes. Add the egg, sugar syrup, brandy, rum, Madeira, and milk, and shake well for about 1 minute. Strain into a goblet and sprinkle with cinnamon. Serve with a cinnamon stick.

Serves 1

Preparation time: 4 minutes

baltimore eggnog

brandy sour

Put the ice cubes into a cocktail shaker. Shake the bitters over the ice, add the lemon juice, brandy, and sugar syrup, and shake until a frost forms. Strain into a tumbler and decorate with lemon slices on a cocktail stick. Serve with a straw.

4–5 ice cubes

3 drops Angostura bitters

juice of 1 lemon

3 measures brandy

1 teaspoon sugar syrup

lemon slices, to decorate

Serves 1

Preparation time: 4 minutes

4–5 ice cubes

3 drops Angostura bitters

½ measure pineapple juice

½ measure blue Curaçao

2 measures brandy

orange zest strip, to decorate

Put the ice cubes into a mixing glass. Shake the bitters over the ice and add the pineapple juice, Curaçao, and brandy. Stir until frothy, then strain into a chilled cocktail glass. Decorate with a strip of orange zest tied into a knot.

Serves 1

Preparation time: 3 minutes

east india

brandy cuban

Place the ice cubes in a tumbler and pour the brandy and lime juice over them. Stir to mix. Top up with cola, and decorate with a lime slice. Drink through a straw.

2–3 ice cubes

1½ measures brandy

juice of ½ lime

cola

lime slice, to decorate

Serves 1

Preparation time: 3 minutes

■ This cocktail is named after Bobby Jones, the American golfer whose heyday was in the 1920s and '30s. He is regarded as the greatest amateur player of all time.

Put the ice cubes into a cocktail shaker. Pour the lemon juice, grenadine, crème de cacao, and brandy over the ice and shake until a frost forms. Strain into a tumbler and serve with a straw.

4–5 ice cubes
juice of 1 lemon
½ teaspoon grenadine
1 measure crème de cacao
3 measures brandy

Serves 1

Preparation time: 3 minutes

bobby jones

monte rosa

Put the ice cubes into a mixing glass. Pour the lime juice, Cointreau, and brandy over the ice, and stir vigorously. Strain into two chilled cocktail glasses.

Pictured Left

4–5 ice cubes

juice of ½ lime

1 measure Cointreau

3 measures brandy

Serves 2

Preparation time: 3 minutes

coffee flip

Put 4–5 ice cubes into a cocktail shaker. Pour in the brandy, Kahlúa, cream, and sugar syrup, then add the egg, coffee, and milk, and shake well for 45 seconds. Put the remaining ice cubes into a tall glass, strain the drink over the ice and sprinkle with ground coriander.

Pictured Right

8–10 ice cubes

1 measure brandy

1 measure Kahlúa

2 teaspoons heavy cream

1½ teaspoons sugar syrup

1 egg, beaten

½ teaspoon instant coffee

4 oz. milk

ground coriander, to decorate

Serves 1

Preparation time: 4 minutes

Kahlúa is a coffee-based liqueur from Mexico. Among its other flavorings are vanilla and herbs.

vodka sazerac •

moscow mule •

vodka martini •

sea breeze •

vodka twister fizz •

down-under fizz •

harvey wallbanger •

hawaiian vodka •

vodka

vodka sazerac

Put the sugar cube into an old fashioned glass and shake the bitters onto it. Add the Pernod to the glass and swirl it around so that it clings to the side of the glass. Drop in the ice cubes and pour in the vodka. Top up with the lemon-flavored soda, then stir gently and serve.

1 sugar cube

2 drops Angostura bitters

3 drops Pernod

2–3 ice cubes

2 measures vodka

lemon-flavored soda

Serves 1

Preparation time: 4 minutes

This drink is one of those happy accidents. It was invented in 1941 by an employee of a U.S. drinks firm in conjunction with a Los Angeles bar owner who was overstocked with ginger beer. It was originally served in a copper mug.

3–4 cracked ice cubes
2 measures vodka
juice of 2 limes
ginger beer
lime and orange slices, to decorate

Serves 1

Preparation time: 4 minutes

Put the cracked ice into a cocktail shaker. Add the vodka and lime juice and shake well. Pour into a hurricane glass, top up with ginger beer and stir gently. Decorate with lime and orange slices and serve with straws.

moscow mule

vodka martini

Put the ice cubes into a mixing glass.
Pour the vermouth and vodka over
the ice and stir vigorously, without
splashing. Strain into a chilled cocktail
glass, drop in the olive, and serve.

4–5 ice cubes

¼ measure dry vermouth

3 measures vodka

1 green olive

Serves 1
Preparation time: 3 minutes

This is one of those drinks that has changed considerably over the years. In the 1930s it was made with gin rather than vodka and with grenadine and lemon juice instead of cranberry juice and grapefruit juice.

1 measure vodka

1½ measures cranberry juice

1½ measures fresh grapefruit juice

5 ice cubes, crushed

lime slice, to decorate

Put the vodka, cranberry juice, and grapefruit juice into a tall glass with the crushed ice and stir well. Decorate with a lime slice and drink through a straw.

sea breeze

Serves 1
Preparation time: 3 minutes

vodka twister fizz

Put the ice cubes into a cocktail shaker. Pour the lemon juice, sugar syrup, egg white, Pernod, and vodka over the ice, and shake until a frost forms. Pour without straining into a highball glass, and top up with ginger ale. Stir once or twice, decorate with a lime slice, and serve.

Pictured Left

4–5 ice cubes

juice of 1 lemon

½ teaspoon sugar syrup

1 egg white

3 drops Pernod

3 measures vodka

ginger ale

lime slice, to decorate

Serves 1

Preparation time: 4 minutes

down-under fizz

Put the ice cubes into a cocktail shaker. Pour the lemon and orange juices, grenadine, and vodka over the ice, and shake until a frost forms. Pour without straining into a Collins glass, and top up with club soda. Serve with a straw.

Pictured Right

4–5 ice cubes

juice of 1 lemon

juice of ½ orange

½ teaspoon grenadine

3 measures vodka

club soda

Serves 1

Preparation time: 3 minutes

harvey wallbanger

Put half the ice cubes, the vodka, and orange juice into a cocktail shaker. Shake well for about 30 seconds, then strain into a tall glass over the remaining ice cubes. Float the Galliano on top. Decorate with orange slices and serve with straws.

6 ice cubes

1 measure vodka

4 oz. fresh orange juice

1–2 teaspoons Galliano

orange slices, to decorate

Serves 1

Preparation time: 3 minutes

A drink from the 1960s, the Harvey Wallbanger is said to have been named after a California surfer who drank so much of it that as he found his way out of the bar he banged and bounced from one wall to the other.

4–5 ice cubes

1 measure pineapple juice

juice of 1 lemon

juice of 1 orange

1 teaspoon grenadine

3 measures vodka

lemon slice, to decorate

Put the ice cubes into a cocktail shaker. Pour the pineapple, lemon, and orange juices, grenadine, and vodka over the ice and shake until a frost forms. Strain into a tumbler and decorate with a slice of lemon. Drink with a straw.

Serves 1
Preparation time: 3 minutes

hawaiian vodka

kir •

wine cooler •

classic champagne cocktail •

caribbean champagne •

millennium cocktail •

bellinitini •

champagne
& wine

kir

Put the ice cubes into a goblet or an old fashioned glass. Pour the crème de cassis and wine over the ice, stir gently, and serve.

Pictured Left

2–3 ice cubes

1 measure crème de cassis

4 measures dry white wine

Serves 1
Preparation time: 3 minutes

Crème de cassis is a black currant-based liqueur from Dijon that blends deliciously with dry white wine. In French bars this drink is sometimes called vin blanc cassis and sometimes Kir.

wine cooler

Put the ice cubes into a goblet or tumbler. Pour the elderflower cordial and the wine over the ice, then top up with club soda. Decorate with the lemon zest spiral, stir, then serve.

Pictured Right

4–5 ice cubes

1 measure elderflower cordial

4 measures white wine

club soda

lemon zest spiral, to decorate

Serves 1
Preparation time: 3 minutes

classic champagne cocktail

Put the sugar cube into a champagne glass or cocktail glass, and saturate it with the bitters. Add the brandy and Cointreau, then fill the glass with champagne. Serve decorated with an orange slice.

1 sugar cube

2–3 drops Angostura bitters

½ teaspoon brandy

½ teaspoon Cointreau

4 measures chilled champagne

orange slice, to decorate

Serves 1

Preparation time: 2 minutes

If you have time, leave the sugar cube in the glass for up to 45 minutes after you have soaked it with the bitters. It will improve the flavor no end.

A splash of Angostura bitters enlivens many cocktails. The pink element in a pink gin, it was first made in the Venezuelan town of Angostura during the nineteenth century, but is now produced in Trinidad.

1 tablespoon light rum
1 tablespoon crème de bananes
dash of Angostura bitters
chilled champagne or sparkling wine

To Decorate:
slice of banana
slice of pineapple
maraschino cherry

Pour the rum, crème de bananes, and bitters into a chilled champagne flute. Top up with champagne and stir gently. Decorate with the banana and pineapple slices, and cherry, all speared on a cocktail stick.

Serves 1

Preparation time: 3 minutes

caribbean champagne

millennium cocktail

Put the ice cubes into a cocktail shaker, add the vodka, raspberry and orange juices, and shake thoroughly. Strain into a champagne glass and pour in the chilled champagne.

4–5 ice cubes

1 measure vodka

1 measure fresh raspberry juice

1 measure fresh orange juice

4 measures champagne or sparkling dry white wine, chilled

Serves 1

Preparation time: 3 minutes

4–5 ice cubes

2 measures vodka

½ measure peach schnapps

1 teaspoon peach juice

champagne

Put the ice cubes, vodka, peach schnapps, and peach juice into a cocktail shaker, and shake thoroughly. Strain into a chilled cocktail glass and top up with champagne.

Serves 1
Preparation time: 3 minutes

bellinitini

non-alcoholic drinks

½ cup sugar syrup

1½ cups fresh lemon juice

1 quart apple juice

ice cubes

2½ quarts ginger ale

orange slices, to decorate

Stir together the sugar syrup and
lemon and apple juices in a large
chilled jug. Add the ice cubes and
pour in the ginger ale. Decorate with
orange slices and serve.

Serves 25–30

Preparation time: 10 minutes

prohibition punch

carrot cream

Put the carrot juice, cream, egg yolks, and orange juice into a cocktail shaker and shake well. Divide the ice cubes among 4 tall glasses and pour the carrot drink on top. Decorate with orange slices and serve immediately. Drink with straws.

1 cup carrot juice

1¼ cups light cream

4 egg yolks

½ cup fresh orange juice

20 ice cubes

orange slices, to decorate

Serves 4

Preparation time: 4 minutes

Carrot juice and orange juice blend very well in this delicious and nutritious drink.

grapefruit mint cooler

Put the sugar and water into a heavy-based pot and stir over a low heat until dissolved. Leave to cool. Crush the mint leaves and stir them into the syrup. Cover and leave to stand for about 12 hours, then strain into a jug. Add the lemon and grapefruit juices to the strained syrup and stir well. Fill 6 old fashioned glasses or tumblers with crushed ice, and pour the cocktail into the glasses. Pour in the club soda and decorate with mint sprigs.

½ cup sugar

½ cup water

handful of mint leaves

juice of 4 large lemons

2 cups fresh grapefruit juice

crushed ice

1 cup club soda

mint sprigs, to decorate

Serves 6

Preparation time: 10 minutes plus standing

To make a Cranberry Mint Cooler, substitute cranberry juice for the grapefruit juice.

3 ice cubes

1 measure fresh orange juice

1 measure fresh lemon juice

1 measure pineapple juice

1 measure fresh grapefruit juice

2 dashes grenadine

1 egg white

club soda

To Decorate:

lemon slice

lime slice

maraschino cherry

orange zest spiral

Serves 1	
Preparation time: 4 minutes	

Put the ice cubes into a cocktail shaker and pour in the orange, lemon, pineapple, and grapefruit juices, grenadine, and egg white. Shake well, then strain into a large goblet. Top up with club soda and decorate with the lemon and lime slices, the maraschino cherry on a cocktail stick, and an orange zest spiral. Drink through a straw.

san francisco

index

Special Photography:
Neil Mersh
Jacket Photography:
Neil Mersh
Cocktail Preparation:
Ben & Paul
The Salmon & Compasses
58 Penton Street
London
N1 9PZ